GREEK!

Alison Hawes

Some of the activities in this book may require adult help.
An asterix (*) indicates that adult supervision is needed.

Published 2010 by
A & C Black Publishers Ltd.
36 Soho Square, London, W1D 3QY

www.acblack.com

ISBN   HB   978-1-4081-2433-8
        PB   978-1-4081-2690-5

Series consultant: Gill Matthews

Text copyright © 2010 Alison Hawes

The right of Alison Hawes to be identified as the author of this work has been asserted by her in accordance with the Copyrights, Designs and Patents Act 1988.

A CIP catalogue for this book is available from the British Library.

Every effort has been made to trace copyright holders and to obtain their permission for use of copyright material. The authors and publishers would be pleased to rectify any error or omission in future editions.

This book is produced using paper that is made from wood grown in managed, sustainable forests. It is natural, renewable and recyclable. The logging and manufacturing processes conform to the environmental regulations of the country of origin.

Produced for A & C Black by Calcium. www.calciumcreative.co.uk

Printed and bound in China by C&C Offset Printing Co.

All the internet addresses given in this book were correct at the time of going to press. The author and publishers regret any inconvenience caused if addresses have changed or sites have ceased to exist, but can accept no responsibility for any such changes.

Acknowledgements

The publishers would like to thank the following for their kind permission to reproduce their photographs:

Cover: DK Images: Liz McAulay; Shutterstock **Pages:** Alamy Images: Ivy Close Images 18b; Alison Hawes: 5bl, 5bc, 7, 9, 11b, 13, 15, 17, 19, 21, 23, 25, 27, 29b; Fotolia: Denis Topal 6l; Istockphoto: Ulrich Schendzielorz 14t; The Ohio Statehouse Photo Archive: 16; Photolibrary: Gimmi Gimmi 24r; Shutterstock: Danilo Ascione 28b, Clara 28t, Panos Karapanagiotis 11t, 12r, Kompasstudio 4, Krechet 5t, Laurelie 30, Ninette Luz 2–32, Georgy Markov 20r, Ivan Montero Martinez 10, Maxstockphoto 18t, Michaela Stejskalova 8t, Florin Tirlea 8b; Wikimedia: Matthias Kabel 24l, Grant Mitchell 26t, Marie-Lan Nguyen 12l, 14b, 20l, 22b, 26b, Bibi Saint-Pol 6r, 22t, 29t. **Map:** Geoff Ward.

Contents

Go Greek!

The ancient Greeks

The ancient Greeks lived thousands of years ago, in the country we now know as Greece. But you can see from this map that they also lived in parts of Italy and Turkey, and beyond.

Athens, the capital city of Greece.

The places marked in orange on this map show where the ancient Greeks lived.

Archaeology

We know a lot about the ancient Greeks because archaeologists have found the remains of the temples, theatres, and ships the Greeks built. They have also discovered many smaller items such as pottery, jewellery, money, and toys.

Have fun making your own ancient Greek items.

Activities

As well as information about the ancient Greeks, this book gives you instructions for different activities that you can do at home or at school. Enjoy the activities but DON'T FORGET:

- Read all the instructions before you begin.

- Protect yourself and the surface you are working on. (Some of the activities in the book are messy!)

- Always tidy up after you have completed an activity.

- Always ask for adult help when you see this **symbol**: *

5

The ancient Greeks were famous for making beautiful clay pots. We can learn a lot about the ancient Greeks from their pottery, because they often decorated their pots with scenes from their everyday lives.

Pots with black pictures were first made in Corinth, around 700 BC.

The fashion for pots with red pictures began in Athens, in 530 BC.

Make your own Greek pot

You will need:

• *an old dinner plate* • *cling film* • *short strips of newspaper and white paper* • *paste and paste brush* • *poster paints and paint brush* • *PVA glue*

1 Cover the upturned plate with cling film.

2 Paste four layers of newspaper on top of this and leave to dry.

3 Paste two layers of white paper on top of this and again leave to dry.

4 Remove the china plate and cling film.

5 Paste two layers of white paper on the inside of your paper plate.

6 When dry, paint a picture on your plate.

7 Finally, make your plate shiny by painting on a layer of PVA glue.

This finished plate has an ancient Greek design.

Shapes and sizes

About 20 different shapes were used to make ancient Greek pots.

Look at the shape of the pot and see what it was used for.

Storing wine and oil

Collecting water

Pouring

Drinking

7

Food

The ancient Greeks ate very healthily. They ate lots of fruit and vegetables, bread, oatmeal, and sometimes fish. Only rich people could afford to eat a lot of meat.

The Greeks grew grapes to eat and also to make wine.

Ancient Greek menu

Breakfast:
Bread dipped in wine

Lunch:
Bread, cheese, and fruit

Dinner:
Porridge or beans, and vegetables and bread.

Pasteli is an ancient Greek sweet made with honey and **sesame**.

The ancient Greeks used honey to sweeten their food. They kept their bees in clay hives.

Ask an adult for help when you see this sign.

Make your own pasteli*

You will need:

- *150 g (5 oz) runny honey*
- *150 g (5 oz) sesame seeds*
- *a piece of lemon rind*
- *20 cm (8 in) square baking tin (lined with greaseproof paper)*
- *a medium saucepan*
- *kitchen scissors and wooden spoon*

1 Heat the honey in the pan until it starts to boil.

2 Stir in the lemon rind and the sesame seeds.

3 Simmer for a few minutes, stirring all the time.

4 Switch off the heat and remove the lemon rind.

5 Spread the mixture evenly in the tin and refrigerate for two hours.

6 Cut the pasteli into squares with kitchen scissors.

7 Peel off the paper and eat!

Store your pasteli on a plate in the fridge.

NOW TRY THIS!

The ancient Greeks cooked over an open fire – but you can use a cooker. Find more ancient Greek recipes at:

www.greek-recipe.com/static/ancient/ancientrecipes.html

and cook an ancient Greek meal for your friends.

Theatre

The ancient Greeks built many outdoor theatres. They went to the theatre to see plays, music, and dancing.

Actors in Greek plays wore masks. The masks showed the audience the kind of character the actor was playing. Plays from ancient Greece are still sometimes performed today.

No women!

All the actors in ancient Greek plays were men. So they played the women's roles too.

This theatre in Epidaurus, in Greece, held about 14,000 people.

Make your own theatre mask*

You will need:

• *a balloon* • *cling film* • *a small roll of modroc (plaster bandages) cut into short lengths* • *scissors* • *poster paints and paint brush* • *pencil*

1. Blow up the balloon to the size of your head.

2. Wrap the balloon in cling film.

3. Dip the modroc pieces, one at a time into water and cover one side of the balloon with two layers of modroc.

4. Let the mask dry and discard the balloon and cling film.

5. Draw eyes and a mouth on the mask and cut them out.

6. Add one more layer of modroc to your mask.

7. Then add more modroc to make eyebrows, lips, cheeks and a nose that stand out from the face.

8. Leave to dry before painting.

Greek plays were either tragedies or comedies. This mask is designed for a Greek tragedy.

Tie a length of thin elastic to your finished mask before trying it on.

Almost every year, a big sports festival was held somewhere in ancient Greece. The most famous festival was the **Olympic Games** held at Olympia. Only men were allowed to take part. Women weren't even allowed to watch.

Athletics was a favourite Greek sport.

Winners of sports competitions were often awarded a victory wreath and wool ribbons.

Make your own victory wreath*

You will need:

- *medium garden wire*
- *green insulating tape*
- *green paper*
- *scissors*

1 Measure your head and cut twice this length of garden wire.

2 Form the wire into a double ring.

3 Wrap the tape round the ring, until the wire is hidden.

4 Cut 40 life-size leaves with stalks from the green paper.

5 Starting at the top, tape a leaf to the wire by its stalk.

6 Then working backwards down one side of the ring, tape on more leaves, overlapping each one with the one before.

7 When you have covered half of the ring, go back up to the top and cover the rest of the ring with leaves.

This finished wreath is made of paper and wire. In ancient Greece it would have been made of leaves.

For women

Women had their own sports festival. It was held in honour of the goddess, Hera.

Home Life

In ancient Greece, men and women led separate lives. Even at home, there were often separate rooms for men and women.

All families used oil lamps to light their home.

Women and girls were expected to spend most of their time at home. Women that came from rich families had slaves to do most household chores for them. Women from poor families had to do all the work themselves.

It was a woman's job to spin and weave the cloth needed for her family's clothes.

Make your own oil lamp*

You will need:

- *300 g (10 oz) of self hardening clay*
- *a work board*
- *clay tools*
- *cling film*

1 Wrap a quarter of the clay in cling film.

2 Roll the remaining clay into a ball.

3 Flatten the ball slightly and then push both your thumbs into the middle.

4 Then hollow out the middle of the ball with your hands.

5 As you work, make a handle at one end of the lamp and a lip for the nozzle at the other end.

6 When the base is ready, roll the quarter of clay into a ball.

7 Roll it out into a thick circle to make a "lid" for your lamp.

8 Make a hole in the "lid" with a straw.

9 Join the "lid" to the base with your fingers.

10 Leave your lamp to dry completely.

Light your lamp*

Pour a little olive oil into the lamp. Push a wick into the nozzle and light with a match.

Law

The ancient Greeks first introduced the idea of having a **jury** in a court of law. A water clock was used in the **lawcourts** to limit the time people could speak.

Being on a jury

In Athens, citizens were expected to serve on a jury. To serve on a jury you had to:

- be born in Athens
- be over 30 years old
- be a man

The jury voted whether someone was guilty or innocent of a crime. **Jurors** were given two **ballot** tokens to vote with.

Democratic Greece

All men in ancient Greece could vote. The system in which all citizens can vote is called "democracy". It was introduced by Cleisthenes (above). However, only men could vote in ancient Greece.

Make your own ballot tokens

You will need:

- *a plastic bottle top*
- *thick card*
- *a drinking straw*
- *self hardening clay*
- *bronze paint and paint brush*
- *single hole puncher*

1 Draw round a poker chip, twice on thick card.

2 Cut out these circles and punch a hole in the centre of each one.

3 Cut two pieces of drinking straw, each 5 cm (2 in) long.

4 Push a cut straw half way through each circle.

5 Plug both ends of one straw with clay and leave to dry.

6 Give each token three coats of bronze paint.

The ballot token with a hollow centre (on the right) was used for a guilty vote. The one with a solid centre (on the left) was for a not guilty vote.

NOW TRY THIS!

Ancient Greek juries had hundreds of members. Find out how many people are on a jury today. Is it the same as it was in Athens?

The ancient Greeks thought education was important. Wealthy families sent their boys to schools when they were seven. Boys studied reading, writing, maths, music, poetry, and sport. They wrote on **wax tablets**. Poor boys didn't often go to school and girls were taught at home by their mothers.

Ancient Greeks wrote on scrolls made of **papyrus** or animal skin.

This piece of a pot shows students and their teachers. The students are being taught to read and to play music.

18

Make your own scroll*

You will need:

- *a broom handle*
- *a saw*
- *4 wooden door knobs*
- *wood glue*
- *a short roll of paper*
- *cold tea*
- *double sided sticky tape*
- *sandpaper*
- *kitchen roll*

1 Cut two 23 cm (9 in) rollers from the broom handle.

2 Smooth the ends of the rollers with sandpaper.

3 Glue the door knobs to the rollers and leave overnight.

4 Make a pot of strong tea and leave to go cold.

5 Pour the tea into a bowl and dip the paper in for a few seconds.

6 Let the paper dry on kitchen roll, overnight.

7 Attach the paper to the rollers with sticky tape.

Roll up your finished scroll when not in use and secure it with a ribbon or elastic band.

NOW TRY THIS!

Use the link below to copy the Greek alphabet on to your scroll or try writing your name in Greek letters:

http://www.schoolhistory. co.uk/primarylinks/ancient greeceresources/greece17.pdf

Ancient Greeks wore two main pieces of clothing – a tunic and a cloak. Tunics could be short or long and were fastened at the shoulders. They were usually made of cotton or silk.

Cloaks were wrapped around the body or pinned at one shoulder.

The tunics worn by women were usually longer than those worn by men.

20

Make your own Greek clothes

You will need:

- *1 m to 1.5 m (3 to 4½ ft) of fabric for the cloak and a large rectangle of fabric for the tunic*
- *4 to 6 large press stud fasteners (poppers)*
- *2 m (6 ft) of coloured cord*
- *needle and thread*
- *scissors*
- *thick card*
- *bronze acrylic paint and paint brush*
- *PVA glue and paste brush*

1 Measure
   a) the distance between your wrists, then double it.
   b) the distance from your shoulder to your feet.

2 Cut a rectangle of fabric matching these measurements and fold it in half widthways.

3 Sew up the side seam.

4 Sew poppers along the top edge, spacing them so there is room for your arms and head, when fastened.

5 Glue small circles of bronze painted card, on top of the poppers and leave to dry.

6 Put the tunic on and tie the cord around your waist.

7 Pull some of the tunic up, so it hangs over the cord belt.

8 To make the cloak, fold the fabric lengthways and wrap it around your body, fastening it at the shoulder with a brooch or popper.

This tunic is called a chiton.

Toys and Games

Ancient Greek children liked to play games and take part in sport. Younger children may have played with toys like a spinning top. Spinning tops were made from clay or wood. They were spun with a strip of leather.

Older children may have played with toys like yo-yos or marbles. They especially loved games with scary names, like "knucklebones".

This plate shows a Greek child playing with a yo-yo.

Ths pull-along toy from ancient Greece is over 2,500 years old.

Make your own knucklebones game

You will need:

- *25 g (1 oz) of self hardening clay*
- *work board*
- *clay tools*
- *white or cream paint*

1 Cut the clay into 5 pieces and roll each one into a ball.

2 Using your fingers, slightly flatten and squeeze each ball into a knuckle bone shape.

3 Using the clay tools, mark the knucklebones with dents and ridges (like the knucklebones in the photograph above right).

4 Leave the "bones" to dry completely.

5 Give the knucklebones three coats of white or cream paint.

The ancient Greeks used ankle bones from sheep and goats as "knucklebones". They also made them from clay, like the ones above.

NOW TRY THIS!

No one is quite sure how the ancient Greeks played knucklebones. But it is thought the rules may have been like those for Fives or Jacks.

Visit www.mastersgames.com/rules/jacks-rules.htm to find out how to play and challenge a friend to a game.

Nowhere in Greece is far from the sea. So it is not surprising that the ancient Greeks became great sailors and ship builders. In the 6th century BC, the ancient Greeks invented a new warship called a trireme. They were powered by sails and 170 oarsmen.

Protective eye

Many ships had a large eye painted on the **prow**. Ancient Greeks believed it protected their ship from bad luck and from their enemies.

Triremes had a long metal spike on their prow, to use as a **battering ram** against enemy ships.

Greek ships took olive oil, pots, and wine to countries all around the Mediterranean sea.

Make your own protective eye

You will need:

- *poster paints and paint brush*
- *a large paper plate*
- *a piece of ribbon*
- *sticky tape*
- *thick black marker pen*

Bold colours and a dark outline make the eye stand out.

1. Paint a large eye in the centre circle of the plate.

2. Paint a plain background around the eye.

3. Paint the border of the plate in a different colour.

4. When the border is dry, draw a pattern on it with the marker pen.

5. Outline the eye with the marker pen.

6. Tape a loop of ribbon on to the back of the plate and hang it in your room.

This plate has a "key" pattern. The design was very popular in ancient Greece.

NOW TRY THIS!

Did you know there was nowhere to sleep or eat on a trireme? Watch a great video about triremes at:

www.youtube.com/watch?v=A46UCkZRnoM&NR=1

then find out more about triremes at:

www.historyforkids.org/learn/greeks/science/sailing/warships.htm

Greek men were expected to serve in the army. Most fought as foot soldiers called hoplites.

Hoplite soldiers marched into battle with their shields overlapping and their spears ready to throw.

To protect his body a soldier wore a helmet, a **cuirass**, and **greaves** and carried a large shield.

Make your own hoplite shield

You will need:

- *a large sheet of thick white card*
- *a large sheet of thin black card*
- *PVA glue and paste brush*
- *poster paints and brush*
- *scissors*
- *paper clips*

1 Cut out a 51 cm (20 in) wide circle, from the white card, for the shield.

2 Draw 2 circles, one inside the other, on the shield. Make one 45 cm (17 in) wide and the other 41 cm (16 in) wide.

3 Paint a design in the centre of your shield.

4 Paint the border between the 41 cm (16 in) and 45 cm (17 in) circles and leave to dry.

5 Cut flaps at 5 cm (2 in) intervals, from the edge of the 51 cm (20 in) circle to the edge of the 45 cm (17 in) circle and fold them back.

6 Glue a strip of black card to the flaps to form a rim around the shield. Hold the strip in place with paper clips until dry.

7 Glue a short strip of card to the inside of the shield to make a handle and leave to dry.

The painting on this finished card shield shows the snake-haired Medusa from Greek legends.

Myths and Legends

The ancient Greeks told countless stories about their gods and heroes. We know these myths and legends today, because the Greeks wrote them down.

Some Greek myths can also be seen painted as a **frieze** on a pot or carved into stone.

One of the most famous Greek legends tells how the hero **Perseus** killed the snake-haired Medusa (above).

There are many stories of the Greek hero, **Hercules**. This statue shows him fighting a centaur.

Make your own story frieze

You will need:

- *a book of Greek myths and legends*
- *some A5 sheets of white paper*
- *felt tips*
- *coloured backing paper*
- *scissors*
- *glue stick*

1 Choose your favourite Greek myth or legend.

2 Decide on four or five important scenes to tell your story.

3 Draw each scene on one of the A5 sheets.

4 Colour your pictures with felt tips.

5 Mount the finished frieze on the backing paper.

6 Decorate the border with a Greek pattern copied from a vase.

This Greek pot shows brave Theseus about to kill the Minotaur.

THESEUS SAILS TO CRETE

ARIADNE GIVES THESEUS A BALL OF STRING

THESEUS GOES INTO THE MAZE

THESEUS KILLS THE MINOTAUR

The story in this frieze shows how Theseus sailed to Crete to defeat the Minotaur.

Glossary

ballot a vote

battering ram a thick, heavy pole used to break through an enemy's defences

cuirass bronze or leather armour protecting the upper body

frieze a picture or decoration running round the sides of a pot or a building

greaves leg protectors

Hercules in Greek myths, he was the strongest man on Earth

jurors people who serve on a jury

jury a group of people who decide whether someone is innocent or guilty in a lawcourt

lawcourt a building or room where a judge and jury make their decision

Medusa a female monster with snakes for hair who turned those who looked at her into stone

myths ancient stories about gods, goddesses and heroes

Olympic Games in ancient Greece, these games were held every four years for five days, held in honour of Zeus

papyrus a type of paper made from plant stems

Perseus in Greek myths he was the son of Zeus (King of the Greek gods)

prow the front, pointed end of a ship

sesame a plant with tiny edible seeds

symbol a pattern or picture

wax tablet a piece of wood with a wax covering, on which people wrote

wreath a ring of leaves or flowers worn on the head

Further Information

Websites

Explore ancient Greece at:
www.ancientgreece.co.uk

Discover information, photos, and links to more websites at:
www.woodlands-junior.kent.sch.uk/Homework/Greece.html

You'll find information, stories, timeline, and resources at:
www.bbc.co.uk/schools/primaryhistory/ancient_greeks

Books

The Greeks by Abigail Wheatley. Usborne Children's Books (2004).

The Traveller's Guide to Ancient Greece by Fiona MacDonald. Marshall Publishers (1998).

Places to visit

British Museum, London
This museum has many rooms of items from ancient Greece. Room 69 is a good place to start. You can also take a virtual tour of the rooms via the British Museum website.

Index